A Popular Guide

to

Suffolk Place-names

by James Rye

Published and typeset by

The Larks Press
Ordnance Farmhouse, Guist Bottom, Dereham,
Norfolk NR20 5PF

01328 829207

Printed by the Lanceni Press, Garrood Drive, Fakenham.

L9103

British Library Cataloguing-in-Publication Data
A catalogue record for this book is available
from the British Library.

ISBN 0 948400 55 2

Acknowledgements

Like all place-name enthusiasts I owe a great debt to Eilert Ekwall whose *Oxford Dictionary of English Place-names* (O.U.P. 1987) is my chief reference work. Ekwall's dictionary was originally published in 1936, and I have used the more recent scholarship of many other authors, notably of A.D.Mills and Margaret Gelling, to supplement Ekwall's work. A full list of sources used is listed in 'Suggested Further Reading' on pages 9 and 10.

My wife, Nina, and my children, Eleanor and Simon, have become used to the strange noises and puzzled mumblings that I make as we drive past sign-posts. Their tolerance of my enthusiasm and their help in the tedious checking through long lists of names has been much appreciated. The mistakes, of course, are mine.

James Rye

Discovering Place-Names

Perhaps 'Ipswich' has always been associated with shopping or football in your mind, 'Newmarket' was where you visited your sick Aunt Maud as a child, and 'Exning' was where you stayed the night with friends. It has never occurred to you that the names actually mean something. However, the names did not just happen because the first people to use them liked the sounds that the words made. Our ancestors chose the names carefully to describe the people, the wildlife, or the countryside where they lived.

Folk Information

Many place-names are derived from the person or group of people who first settled in the area. For example, **Sweden** literally means 'the Swedes'. A less obvious example is **Wales.** This came from an Old English word *wealas* which meant 'foreigners'. To the early Anglo-Saxon invaders, Wales became the place of the foreigners after the invaders had driven many of the original Celtic inhabitants westward. **Wessex** was the area where the West Saxons lived, **Sussex** where the South Saxons lived, **Norfolk** where the Northern People lived and the Southern People inhabited **Suffolk.**

The names of some of the towns and villages of Suffolk are a memorial to the people who travelled from the Continent, some as early as the fifth century, to cut the forests and attempt to make a living out of the land. The earliest of these names usually end in *ing* which is derived from the Old English *ingas* and originally meant 'dependants or relatives' of a certain man.

Exning *Gyxen* + *ingas*   The settlement belonging to *Gyxen's people.

Swefling *Swiftel* + *ingas*   The settlement belonging to *Swiftel's people.

NOTE. Where a word is prefixed by *, either here or in the main list of place-names, it means that the precise spelling of the original word, usually a personal name, is in doubt.

Sometimes the names end in *ingham* or *ington*. This is because *ham* or *tun* meaning 'homestead' and 'farmstead' respectively (see below) have been combined with *ingas*. The result is *ingaham* or *ingatun* meaning 'the homestead/farmstead of the people of ...'

Letheringham	*Leodhere + ingas + ham.*	Homestead belonging to Leodhere's people.
Kedingon	*Cydda + ingas + tun.*	Farmstead belonging to Cydda's people.

Schram (1961) has pointed out that there are a remarkable number of identities or close similarities between the early Anglian names of Norfolk and Suffolk. Both counties have Barningham, Barsham, Brettenham, Elmham, Fakenham, Helmingham, Ingham, Needham, Rougham, Shimpling, Thornham, Tuddenham, and Walsham. Identical, though with slight modern variations, are Ludham (Nf) and Loudham (Sf), Shotesham (Nf) and Shottisham (Sf), Saham (Nf) and Soham (Sf); and there are a number of others where the first element, usually a personal name, can be closely paralleled in the two counties: such are Dalling (Nf) and Dallinghoo (Sf), Framingham (Nf) and Framsden, Framlingham (Sf), Hevingham (Nf) and Heveningham (Sf), Harling (Nf) and Herringfleet (Sf: Herlingaflet DB). It cannot be mere coincidence that the similarities and identities are almost entirely among the three types -ing, -ham, and -ingham; these may be regarded as constituting a clear proof that the two counties, making up the Kingdom of East Anglia, formed a distinct linguistic as well as an ethnic unit from the earliest centuries of the Anglo-Saxon period.

Habitation Information

Many place-names contain an element meaning something like 'farm, homestead, enclosure'. As the settlements grew in size the same elements came to mean something like 'village' and later on even 'town'.

ham	first meant 'homestead'.
tun	first meant 'enclosure' or even 'fence'. Later it came to mean 'enclosure round a homestead, a farm' and then 'village'.
by	meant 'homestead' or 'farmstead' then 'village'.
thorp(e)	usually meant a secondary or outlying farm attached to some other settlement.

These words meaning 'some form of habitation' were combined with a variety of other elements to give more precise information about a place.

Ashby	*askr + by.*	Farmstead at the ash-trees.
Westhorpe	*vestr + thorp.*	Westerly outlying farmstead.
Stanton	*stan + tun.*	Stony farmstead.
Gisleham	*Gysela + ham.*	Gysela's homestead.

Nature Information

Some place-names give information about the natural features of the area. We find references to a range of flora. There were alder trees, ash trees, aspens, barley fields, beans, bent-grass, box-trees, beech, quite a lot of broom (as in Norfolk), pollarded and natural oak trees, corn fields, elms, hawthorns, oat fields, cress, leeks, flax, orach (goosefoot family), nettles, pears, garlic, reed beds, rye, brushwood, thorn trees, willows, and crosswort.

The fauna is equally diverse. Although horses dominated the references in Norfolk, they are noticeably absent from Suffolk. However, Suffolk did have gadflies, wild cats, swans, woodpeckers, trout, frogs, geese, goats, stags, hawks, wild birds, martens, owls, pigeons, gnats, bullocks and oxen, pigs, wether sheep (castrated rams), wolves, cuckoos, and possibly mules. There are also numerous references to streams, fords, landing-places, mounds, hills, valleys, ridges, meadows, woods, clearings, marshes, and islands.

Much of the original fauna has long since vanished. Farming practices have changed. The woods have been cleared. The marshes have been drained, making the islands disappear, and the streams may have dried up or changed course. Only a few hills retain an obvious link with the past for the modern visitor. The natural world of the County that we drive through today would not be recognisable to the Anglo-Saxon or Scandinavian settlers. However, the place-names they have left us are a kind of time-capsule which reveals secrets of what the traveller would have seen between a thousand and fifteen hundred years ago.

Ousden	*uf + denu*	Owls' valley.
Spexhall	**speoht + halh*	Woodpeckers' corner.
Bramford	*brom + ford*	Broom ford.
Thorndon	*thorn + dun*	Thorn-tree hill.

A Variety of Sources

British place-names contain elements that can be traced back to the languages spoken by at least five quite distinct groups of people. Some of us may have been misled by the victory in World War II into thinking that Britain has never been 'slaved'. However, the truth is very different from what we may want to think. The Welsh, the Scots, and the Irish are well aware that they have often been invaded by the English (amongst others). And a brief excursion into English history will reveal that the country has been invaded by the Celts, the Romans, the Anglo-Saxons, the Scandinavians, and the French. All of these groups contributed words which make up the place-names we have today.

The Celts

The Celts were one of the many tribes living in Europe in the years before Christ. About 400 BC they began to leave Central Europe, possibly because of harassment from other tribes. The Celts from Northern France and the Netherlands crossed the Channel and settled in England. They were known as the Brythons (Britons). Later, about 350 BC, Celts from Southern France settled in Ireland. They spoke *Goidelic* (Gaelic).

The Celts left behind names that are found most abundantly in the North and West (especially Wales and Cornwall). They also gave names to many rivers. Celtic names are often found in isolated spots which suggest that more remote groups remained Celtic-speaking long after other groups had accepted the language of the Anglo-Saxons.

Celtic elements include:

aber	mouth of a river
coombe	a deep valley
glen	a narrow valley
pen	a hill
tor	a hill

There are very few names in Suffolk which contain Celtic elements. Most of the Celts probably fled the area when the Anglo-Saxon invaders arrived along the Eastern coast. Despite the survival of their Anglo-Saxon names, **Walpole** and **Walton** were originally Celtic settlements and the first element of **Dunwich** is possibly linked to the Celtic word for 'deep', meaning something like 'port with deep water'.

4

The Romans

After 300 years of calling the British Isles their own, the Celts were conquered by the Romans. Between 43 AD and 410, England was the north-west corner of the vast Roman Empire. Although the Romans occupied the country for over three centuries, they only left behind approximately 300 place names. This strongly suggests that the Roman administrators tended to use existing Celtic names.

The main Latin elements in place-names are:

castra (-chester, -caster)	a Roman town, fort
colonia (-coln)	a settlement
porta (-port)	a gate
portus (-port)	a harbour
strata (Strat-, -street)	a Roman Road

As with the Celtic elements, there are very few names in Suffolk that contain Latin elements. There are no names containing elements from the pre-Saxon period. A few names contain the much later designations of Magna (Greater) and Parva (Smaller).

The Anglo-Saxons

The Angles, Saxons, and Jutes began to invade the British Isles in 449 AD. They came from Denmark and the coast of Germany and Holland. The Anglo-Saxons named their new country *Englaland* (the land of the Angles) and their language was called *Englisc* (what modern scholars refer to as 'Anglo-Saxon' or 'Old English').

Most place-names in Suffolk were originally given by the Anglo-Saxons. The Old English words that they used in the place-names are far too numerous to list here (see references to A.H.Smith in the suggestions for further reading). I have given a few of the common Old English place-name elements below:

burna (-borne)	a brook, stream
dun	a hill
eg (-ey)	an island
halh	a nook, corner of land
ham	a homestead

hamm	an enclosure, water-meadow
ingas (-ing)	the people of ...
leah (-ley)	a clearing
stede	a place, site of a building
tun	an enclosure, farmstead
well	a well, spring
worth	an enclosure, homestead

Assington, Benhall, Elmswell, and **Wortham** are good Suffolk examples of Old English place-names.

Assington	**As(s)a + ingatun.*	*Assa's Homestead.
Benhall	*beanen + halh.*	Bean Nook.
Elmswell	*elm + wella.*	Elm-trees' spring.
Wortham	*worth + ham.*	Homestead with enclosure.

The Scandinavians

From 789 AD onwards, the Vikings from Denmark and Norway raided most parts of the British Isles. After much savage fighting they eventually settled down to live alongside the Anglo-Saxons. Modern Yorkshire, Derbyshire, Lincolnshire, Leicestershire, Norfolk and Suffolk became subject to Danish rule. The Scandinavian language, 'Old Norse', had the same Germanic roots as Old English so, over the years, the two languages mixed quite well.

There are more Scandinavian names in Norfolk than in Suffolk, reflecting the fact that the early Viking invaders sailed up the River Yare and eventually made some settlements nearby.

Some of the common Scandinavian place-name elements are listed below, although, as with the Old English elements, the Old Norse list does not claim to be anywhere near comprehensive (see references to A.H.Smith in the suggestions for further reading).

by	a farm, then a village
dalr	a dale, valley
garthr	a yard
gil	a ravine
holmr (-holm)	flat ground by a river
lundr	a grove

thorpe	a secondary settlement, farm	
thveit (-thwaite)	a meadow	
toft	a site of a house and outbuildings, a plot of land	

The Scandinavian influence in Suffolk can be seen in **Ashby, Barnby, Risby, Thingoe, Lowestoft**, and possibly **Kettleburgh.**

Ashby	OE *æsc*, or ON *askr* + *by*.	Ash-trees farmstead.
Barnby	ON *Barni*, or *Bjarni* + *by*.	Barni's farmstead.
Lowestoft	ON *Hlothver* + *toft* .	Hlothver's plot of land.

The Norman French

The Normans invaded in 1066 AD, with the result that the language of the English Parliament was French for the next 300 years. However, like the Romans before them, they left a very small legacy of place-names. This is because most of the settlements would have been well established by the time of their invasion. Their presence in Suffolk can occasionally be glimpsed in modern distortions of the names of foreign lords who may have owned land on both sides of the Channel. Thirteenth and fourteenth century lords owned the manors and gave their names to places at **Ashbocking, Carlton Colville, Stonham Aspall, Stowlangtoft,** and **Thorpe Morieux**. **Boulge** comes from an Old French word meaning 'uncultivated ground'.

Proceed with Care

Although driving through lanes trying to guess the meaning of the names on the sign-posts can be very entertaining (if the children are old enough, it is more fun than playing I-Spy) it is not always too productive. Even if you know that *-ham* is probably derived from the Old English word meaning 'homestead', you wouldn't necessarily be able to say for certain that Langham, for example, meant 'something plus homestead'. This is because the Old English *hamm* (water meadow or enclosure) also comes out as 'ham' in modern place-names. Only by looking at early forms can you distinguish between the two, and even then it is not always possible. In this particular case, **Langham** could mean either 'long river meadow/enclosure' or 'long homestead'.

7

Until the early spelling of the name is known (and by 'early' I mean at least the twelfth century or before), it is not possible to see which Celtic, Latin, Old English, Old Norse, or even Old French elements might form the name. Place-name scholars have to hunt through a variety of historical documents in order to record early spellings. The most famous of these sources is the *Domesday Book*.

Let me illustrate the importance of knowing the early spellings of a place. Superficially **Hunston** in Suffolk and **Hunston** in West Sussex appear to be very similar. However, their Domesday spellings reveal important differences.

Hunston (Sf)	*Hunterstuna*	**huntere + tun.*	Hunter's farmstead.
Hunston (W.Sus)	*Hunestan*	*Huna + stan*	Huna's boundary stone.

Similarly, you may be forgiven for thinking that **Stanningfield** contained some reference to 'the people of ...' (*ing*) and that Troston doesn't. Again, their early spellings reveal something very different.

Stanningfield	*Stanfelda*	*stan(en) + feld.*	Stony open ground.
Troston	*Trostingtun*	**Trosta + ingatun.*	Farmstead of *Trosta's people.

However, knowing that you may sometimes be wrong and that you will need to check when you get home, shouldn't stop you having a guess. You should soon begin to get a feel for the way the names can be broken into two or three elements.

Abbreviations

*   This indicates a hypothetical form of the word, that is, although there may be good evidence for its assumed existence in the early languages, it is not recorded in independent use, or is only found in use at a later date.

?   This indicates a best guess as to what the element might have been, or indicates a degree of doubt.

C   Celtic
L   Latin
OE   Old English
OFr   Old French
ON   Old Norse
ME   Middle English

Unless otherwise stated, the date of the early spelling of each name, given in italics beneath the place-name, is 1086 (*Domesday Book*).

Suggested Further Reading

Claiborne, R. (1994) *English: Its Life and Times* London: Bloomsbury.

Cameron, K. (1961) *English Place Names* London: Batsford.

Copley, G.J. (1968) *English Place-Names and Their Origins* Newton Abbot: David & Charles.

Ekwall, E. (1987) *The Concise Oxford Dictionary of English Place-names* Oxford: Oxford University Press.

Gelling, M. (1984) *Place-names in the Landscape* London: Dent.

Harrington, E. (1984) *The Meaning of English Place Names* Belfast: The Blackstaff Press.

Mawer, A. & Stenton, F.M. (1980) *Introduction to the Survey of English Place-Names* (English Place-Name Society Volume I, Part I) Cambridge: Cambridge University Press.

Mills, A.D. (1991) *A Dictionary of Place-names* Oxford: Oxford University Press.

Mitchell, B. (1995) *An Invitation to Old English & Anglo-Saxon England* Oxford: Blackwell.

Reaney, P.H. (1987) *The Origin of English Place Names* London: Routledge & Kegan Paul.

Room, A. (1985) *A Concise Dictionary of Modern Place Names in Great Britain and Ireland* Oxford: Oxford University Press.

Rye, J. (1991) *A Popular Guide to Norfolk Place-names* Guist Bottom: The Larks Press

Schram, O.K. (1961) *'Place-Names' in Norwich and Its Region,* 141-149, (British Association for the Advancement of Science) Norwich: Jarrold.

Smith, A.H. (1987) *English Place-Name Elements* Part One A-IW (English Place-Name Society Volume XXV) Cambridge: Cambridge University Press.

Smith, A.H. (1987) *English Place-Name Elements* Part Two JAFN-YTRI (English Place-Name Society Volume XXVI) Cambridge: Cambridge University Press.

Place-names of Suffolk

Acton
Achetuna
OE *Acca* + OE *tun*. Acca's farmstead. Many Actons mean 'farmstead by the oak trees'. However, in this one, the first element is an OE personal name.

Akenham
Acheham
OE *Aca* + OE *ham*. Aca's homestead.

Alde (River)
OE *ald*. Old. Named after Aldeburgh.

Aldeburgh
Aldeburc
OE *(e)ald* + OE *burgh*. Old (and hence, possibly disused) strong-hold.

Alderton
Alretuna
OE *alor* + OE *tun*. Farmstead by the alder trees.

Aldham
Aldeham
OE *ald* + OE *ham*. Old homestead. There is a possibility that the first element may be a personal name. If this is the case, Aldham would mean 'Ealda's homestead'.

Aldringham
Alrincham
OE *Aldhere* + OE *ingas* + OE *ham*. The homestead belonging to Aldhere's people.

Alpheton
Alflede(s)ton (1204)
OE *Ælfflad* or *Æthelflæd* + OE *tun*. Ælfflad's (female) farmstead.

Ampton
Hametuna
OE *?Amma* + OE *tun*. ?Amma's farmstead.

Ashbocking
(Bokkynge Assh 1411)
OE *æsc*. Place at the ash trees that was owned by the de Bockings in the fourteenth century.

Ashby
Aschebi
OE *æsc* or ON *askr* + ON *by*. Farmstead at the ash-trees.

Ashfield (Great)
Eascefelda
OE *æsc* + OE *feld*. Open land where the ash-trees grow.

Aspall
Aspala
OE *aspen* + OE *halh*. Nook of land overgrown with aspens.

Assington
Asetona
OE **As(s)a* + *ingas* + OE *tun*. Farmstead where *Assa's people live.

Athelington
Alinggeton
OE *ætheling* + OE *tun*. Farmstead where the the princes lived.

Bacton
Bachetuna

OE *Bacca* + OE *tun*. Bacca's farmstead.

Badingham
Badincham

OE **Beada* + *ingas* + OE *ham*. Homestead owned by *Beada's people.

Badwell Ash
Badewell (1254)
Badewelle Asfelde
(13th century)

OE *Bada* + OE *wella*. Bada's spring near the open land where the ash-trees grow. Ash is a shortened form of Ashfield..

Ballingdon
Belindune

OE *bealg* + OE *dun*. Rounded hill.

Bardwell
Berdeuwella

OE **Bearda* + OE *wella*. *Bearda's stream.

Barham
Bercheam

OE *beorg* + OE *ham* or *hamm*. Homestead on a hill.

Barking
Berchingas

OE **Berica* + OE *ingas*. The place of *Berica's people.

Barnardiston
Bernardeston
(1194)

OE *Beornheard* + OE *tun*. Beornheard's farmstead.

Barnby
Barnebei

ON *Barni*, or *Bjarni* + ON *by*. Barni's farmstead. There is a possibility that the first element may be ON *barn* (children). Barnby would then mean something like the farmstead owned by the children(heirs).

Barnham (St George and St Martin) OE *beorn* + OE *ham*. Beorn's
Bernham
(Byornham 1000)

homestead. 'St George' and 'St Martin' are from the designation of the churches.

Barningham
Bernincham

OE *Beorn* + *ingas* + OE *ham*. The homestead belonging to Beorn's people.

Barrow
Baro

OE *bearu*. Place in the wood.

Barsham
Barsham

OE *Bar* + OE *ham*. Bar's place.

Barton (Great)
Bertuna

OE *bere-tun*. Barley farm.

Barton Mills
Bertona

OE *bere-tun*. Barley farm with a mill.

Battisford (Tye)
Betesfort

OE **Bætti* + OE *ford*. *Bætti's ford. 'Tye' is a later affix meaning 'common pasture'.

Bawdsey	OE *Baldhere* + OE *eg*. Baldhere's island.
Baldereseia	
Baylham	OE **begel* + OE *ham* or *hamm*. Homestead
Beleham	or water meadow at the river bend.

Bealings (Great & Little) OE *bel-* or *bel* + OE *ingas*. Place be-
Belinges   longing to people in the glade, or people who live
        by the funeral pyre. Se **Belstead**.

Beccles	OE *bece* + OE *læs*. Place by the stream in the
Becles	pasture. There is a tributary of the River Wave-ney to the west of Beccles.
Beck Row	OE *bece*. Row by a stream.
Bedfield	OE *Beda* + OE *feld*. Beda's open land.
Berdefelda	
Bedingfield	OE *Beda* + *ingas* + OE *feld*. The open land
Bedingfelda	belonging to Beda's people.
Belstead	OE *bel-* or *bel* + OE *stede*. Place in a glade or
Belesteda	place by the funeral pyre. There is a Scan-dinavian word *'bil'* meaning 'interval, interspace'. From this both Ekwall and Mills have deduced that *'bel'* probably meant 'a glade'.
Belton	OE *bel-* or *bel* + OE *tun*. Settlement in a glade
Beletuna	or by the funeral pyre. See **Belstead**.
Benacre	OE *bean* + OE *æcre*. Plot of land where beans
Benagra	are grown.
Benfield (Green)	?OE *bean* + ?OE *feld*. Presumably open land where beans are grown.
Benhall	OE *beanen* + OE *halh*. Nook of land where beans
Benehala	are grown.
Bentley	OE *beonet* + OE *leah*. Clearing where bent grass
Benetleia	grows.
Bergholt, East	OE *beorg* + OE *holt*. Wood on a hill.
Bercolt	
Beyton	OE *Bæga* or *Beage* + OE *tun*. Bæga's (man) or
Begatona	Beage's (woman) farmstead.
Bildeston	ON *Bildr* or *bildr* + OE *tun*. Bildr's farmstead.
Bilestuna	However, Gelling points out that *bildr* (meaning 'angle') may be used to denote a hill in the land-scape, in which case the meaning becomes 'farm-stead on the hill'.

Blackheath	?OE *blæc* or *Blaca* + ?OE *hæth.* Possibly dark-coloured heathland, or Blaca's heath-land.
Blackthorpe	?OE *blæc* or *Blaca* + ?ON *thorpe.* Possibly dark-coloured outlying farm, or Blaca's out-lying farm.
Blakenham (Great & Little)	OE *Blaca* + OE *ham* or *hamm.* Blaca's
Blac(he)ham	homestead or water meadow/ enclosure.
Blaxhall	OE **Blæc* + OE *halh.* *Blæc's nook of land.
Blaccheshala	
Blundeston	OE **Blunt* + OE *tun.* Blunt's farmstead.
Blundeston (1203)	
Blyford	OE *Blithe* + OE *ford.* Ford over the River
Blideforda	Blythe. The OE river name means 'gentle or pleasant one'.
Blythburgh	OE *Blithe* + OE *burgh.* Stronghold on the River
Blideburgh	Blythe.
Bosmere	OE *Bosa* + OE *mere.* Bosa's lake.
Bosemera	
Botesdale	OE *Botwulf* + OE *dæl.* Botwulf's valley.
Botholuesdal (1275)	
Boulge	OFr *bouge.* Uncultivated ground probably
Bulges	covered with heather.
Boxford	OE *box* + OE *ford.* Box-tree ford.
Boxford (12 Century)	
Boxted	OE *boc* or *box* + OE *stede.* Beech-trees or box-
Boesteda	trees place.
Boyton	OE *Boia* + OE *tun.* Boia's farmstead.
Boituna	
Bradfield Combust	OE *brad* + OE *feld.* Broad stretch of open land
Bradefelda	The Middle English word *combust* meant 'burnt'.
Bradfield St Clare	OE *brad* + OE *feld.* Broad stretch of open land.
Bradefelda	The land was owned by the Seyncler family.
Bradfield St George	OE *brad* + OE *feld.* Broad stretch of open land
Bradefelda	'St George' refers to the dedication of the church.
Bradley (Great & Little)	OE *brad* + OE *leah.* Broad clearing.
Bradeleia	
Bradwell	OE *brad* + OE *wella.* Place by the broad stream.
Bradewella	

Braiseworth
Briseworde
OE *briosa* + OE *worth*. Gadfly enclosure. There is a possibility that briosa might be used as a nickname for a man - *Briosa's enclosure.

Bramfield
Brunfelda
OE *brom* + OE *felda*. Open land where broom grows.

Bramford
Branfort
OE *brom* + OE *ford*. Broom ford.

Brampton
Brantuna
OE *brom* + OE *tun*. Farmstead where broom grows.

Brandeston
Brantestona
OE **Brant* + OE *tun*. *Brant's farmstead.

Brandon
Brandona
OE *brom* + OE *dun*. Hill where broom grows.

Brantham
Brantham
OE **Branta* + OE *ham* or *hamm*. *Branta's homestead or water meadow/ enclosure.

Bredfield
Bredefelda
OE *brœdu* + OE *feld*. Broad stretch of open land.

Brent Eleigh
Illeleia
(Brendeylleye 1312)
OE **Illa* + OE *leah*.* Illa's clearing in the wood. The ME 'brende' means 'burnt, destroyed

Brettenham
Bretenhama
OE **Bretta* or **Beorhta* + OE *ham*. Bretta's or *Beorhta's homestead.

Bricett (Great)
Brieseta
Possibly OE *briosa* + OE *(ge)set*. Fold infected with gadflies.

Brightwell
Brihtewella
OE *beorht* + OE *wella*. Clear spring.

Brockford
Brocfort
OE *broc* + OE *ford*. Ford over the brook.

Brockley
Broclega
OE *broc* + OE *leah*. Clearing in woodland by a brook. Not to be confused with Brockley in Avon which may have been associated with badgers.

Brome
Brom
OE *brom*. Place where broom grows (in abundance.)

Bromeswell
Bromeswella
OE *brom* + OE *swelle* or *wella*. Broom hill (swelling) or stream where broom grows. Broom hill is most likely.

Bruisyard
Buresiart
OE *(ge)bur* + OE *geard*. Peasant's enclosure.

15

Brundish
Burnedich (1177)
OE *burna* + OE *edisc.* Stream with pasture.

Bucklesham
Bukelesham
OE **Buccel* + OE *ham.* *Buccel's homestead.

Bungay
Bunghea
OE *Buna* + *ingas* + OE *eg.* The island belonging to Buna's people.

Bures
Adburam
OE *bur.* The dwellings or cottages. 'St Mary's' refers to the designation of the Church.

Burgate
Burgata
OE *burg* + OE *geat.* Gate of a fortified settlement.

Burgh
Burc
OE *burg.* Fortified place.

Burgh Castle
Burch
OE *burg.* Fortified place. Probably referring to an old Roman fort.

Burstall
Burgestala
OE *burh-stall.* Site of a fortified settlement.

Bury St Edmunds
Sancte Eadmundes
Byrig (1038)
OE *burh.* Fortified settlement associated with the C9th king of East Anglia, St Eadmund.

Butley
Butelea
OE **Butta* or **butte* + OE *leah.* Butta's clearing, or clearing with a mound or hill.

Buxhall
Buckeshala
OE **Bucc* + OE *halh.* Bucc's corner of land.

Buxlow
Buckeslawe (1250)
OE *Bucc* + OE *hlaw.* Bucc's mound. If the first element is not a personal name, it refers to a male deer

Campsea Ash
Campesseia
Esce
OE *campes* + OE *eg.* Island with a field or enclosure. Ash was originally a separate settlement (OE *aesc* ash-tree).

Capel (St Mary & St Andrew) ME *capel.* St Mary's and St Andrew's
Capeles (1254) chapel.

Carlton (Colville)
Carletuna
Carleton Colvile
(1346)
OE *ceorl* or ON *karl* + OE *tun.* Freemen or peasants' farmstead. The de Colevill family owned the manor in the C13th.

Cattawade
Cattiwad (1247)
OE *catt* + OE *gewæd.* Cats' ford.

Cavendish
Kauanadisc
OE **Cafna* + OE *edisc.* *Cafna's enclosure.

Cavenham *Kanauaham*	OE **Cafna* + OE *ham* or *hamm*. *Cafna's homestead or water meadow/enclosure.
Chadacre *Chearteker (1046)*	OE *ceart* + OE *æcer*. Newly-cultivated land by rough common.
Charsfield *Ceresfelda*	C **car* + OE *feld*. Open land. The first element may be related to a Celtic river name. The place is near a tributary of the Deben.
Chattisham *Cetessam*	OE **Ceatt* + OE *ham* or *hamm*. *Ceatt's homestead or water meadow/enclosure.
Chedburgh *Cedeberia*	OE *Cedda* + OE *beorg*. Cedda's hill.
Chediston *Cedestan*	OE **Cedd* + OE *stan*. *Cedd's stone.
Chelmondiston *Chelmundiston* *(1174)*	OE *Ceolmund* + OE *tun*. Ceolmund's farmstead.
Chelsworth *Cerleswrda*	OE *Ceorl* + OE *worth*. Ceorl's enclosure.
Chevington *Ceuentuna*	OE *Ceofa* + OE *tun*. Ceofa's farmstead.
Chillesford *Cesefortda*	OE *ceosol* + OE *ford*. Gravel ford.
Chilton *Ciltuna*	OE *cilda* + OE *tun*. Literally the 'children's farmstead'. This name is found in several counties (three times in Suffolk) and the first element in this context may be synonymous with 'prince' or 'child of noble birth'. If this is true, the name would mean, 'Young noblemen's farm'.
Clare *Clara*	?C *claear*. This may be a Celtic river-name. It is possibly derived from a Welsh word *claear* meaning 'bright'. The place is on a tributary of the Stour.
Claydon *Clainduna*	OE *clægig* + OE *dun*. Clayey hill.
Clopton *Clopetuna*	OE *clop* + OE *tun*. Farmstead on a hill.
Cockfield *Cochanfelde*	OE **Cohha* + OE *feld*. Cohha's stretch of open land.

Coddenham   OE *Codda + OE ham or hamm.   Codda's home-
  Codenham   stead or water meadow/enclosure.
Combs   OE camb. The ridges, or hill-crests.
  Cambas
Coney Weston   OSc konungr + OE tun. The king's farmstead,
  Cunegestuna   the royal estate. The 'Weston' may be the
                  result of a pronunciation change found in
                  other names where ing becomes ew.
Conyer's Green   This is a relatively modern name. In ME a
                     coninger (sometimes spelled conyer) was a rabbit
                     warren.
Cookley   OE *Cuca + OE leah. *Cuca's clearing.
  Cokelei
Copdock   OE coppede + OE ac. Pollarded oak-tree,
  Coppedoc (1195)   i.e. oak with its top removed.
Cornard (Great, Little) OE corn + OE erth. Cultivated land used for
  Cornerda   growing corn.
Corton   OSc Kari + OE tun. Kari's farmstead.
  Karetuna
Cotton   OE Codda + OE tun. Codda's farmstead.
  Codestuna
Cove (North, South)   OE cofa. Recess or valley. South Cove is close
  Cove,   to the sea and may originally have been a
  Coua   creek on the coast. North Cove is far inland,
           but may have originally been linked with South
           Cove and named from it.
Covehithe   OE hyth. Harbour near (South) Cove.
  Coveheith (1523)
Cowlinge   OE Cul or Cula + OE ingas. Place belonging to
  Cullinge   Cul's or Cula's people.
Cranley   OE cran + OE leah. Cranes' wood.
  Cranlea
Cransford   OE cran + OE ford. Cranes' ford.
  Craneforda
Cratfield   OE *Cræta + OE feld. *Cræta's open land.
  Cratafelda
Creeting (St Mary, St Peter)   OE *Cræta + OE ingas.   Place be-
  Cratingas   longing to *Cræta's people. 'St Mary' and 'St
                Peter' come from the dedication of the churches.

Cretingham
Gratingeham

OE *greot* + OE *ingas* + *ham*. Homestead belonging to the people who live in a sandy or gravelly area.

Crowfield
Crofelda

OE *croh* + OE *feld*. Open land at the nook. The place is at the head of a valley.

Culford
Culeforda

OE *Cula* + OE *ford*. Cula's ford.

Culpho
Culfole

OE **Cuthwulf* + OE *hoh*. *Cuthwulf's spur of land. By the time of the Domesday Book, Cuthwulf had become Cuulf.

Dagworth
Dagaworda

OE *Dæcca* + OE *worth*. Dæcca's enclosure.

Dalham
Dalham

OE *dæl* + OE *ham*. Homestead in a valley.

Dallinghoo
Delingahou

OE *D(e)alla* + OE *ingas* + *hoh*. The spur of land belonging to D(e)alla's people.

Darmsden
Dermodesduna

OE *Deormod* + OE *dun*. Deormod's hill.

Darnford
Derneford

OE *derne* + OE *ford*. Hidden ford.

Darsham
Dersham

OE *Deor* + OE *ham*. Deor's homestead.

Debach
Debenbeis

OE *deopa* + OE *bæce* or *bæc*. Deep valley (*bæce*). Gelling argues for *bæc* meaning 'ridge'. This would give the name meaning 'high ridge' (overlooking the River Deben). The place is in a high situation and is not far from a tributary of the Deben which runs in a deep valley.

Debenham
Depbenham

OE *deope* + OE *ham*. Homestead by the deep river. Ekwall argues that *Deope* 'deep river' may be an OE river name.

Denham
Denham

OE *denu* + OE *ham*. Both the Denham near Eye and the one near Bury St Edmunds mean 'homestead in a valley'.

Dennington
Dingifetuna

OE **Denegifu* + OE *tun*. *Denegifu's (female) farmstead.

Denningworth

OE **Denegifu* + OE *worth*. *Denegifu's enclosure. See **Dennington.**

Denston
Danerdestuna
OE *Deneheard* + OE *tun*. Deneheard's farmstead.

Depden
Depdana
OE *deop* + OE *denu*. Deep valley.

Drinkstone
Drencestuna
OE **Dremic* + OE *tun*. *Dremic's farmstead.

Dunwich
Duneuuic
(Domnoc 636)
C **dubno-* + OE *wic*. A Celtic name, the first element is possibly linked to the Welsh word for 'deep', meaning something like 'port with deep water'. The OE *wic* meaning 'village' or 'harbour' was added later.

Earl Soham
Saham
OE *sæ* + OE *ham*. Homestead by the pool, with early possession by the Earl of Norfolk.

Earl Stonham
See **Stonham Aspall.**

Easton
Estuna
OE *east* + OE *tun*. East farmstead.

Edwardstone
Eduardestuna
OE *Eadweard* + OE *tun*. Eadweard's farmstead.

Ellough
Elga
ON *elgr*. The temple.

Elmham (South &VariousChurches) OE *elm(en)* + OE *ham*. Home-
Almeham
stead where elms grow. 'St Cross', 'St James, 'St Margaret', and 'St Michael' come from the dedication of the churches.

Elmsett
Elmseta
OE *elm* + OE *(ge)set* or *sæte* or *sætan*. Fold, dwelling, or dwellers at the elm trees.

Elmswell
Elmeswella
OE *elm* + OE *wella*. Elm-trees' spring.

Elveden
Eluedena
OE *elfitu* or *elf(a)* + OE *denu*. Swan valley, or Elf valley.

Eriswell
Hereswella
OE **Here* + OE *wella*. *Here's stream.

Erwarton
Eurewardestuna
OE *Eoforweard* + OE *tun*. Eoforweard's farmstead.

Euston
Euestuna
OE *Efe*, or *Eof* + OE *tun*. Efe's or Eof's farmstead.

Exning
Essellinge
(Exningis 1158)
OE **Gyxen* + OE *ingas*. The settlement belonging to *Gyxen's people.

Eye   OE *eg,* or *ieg.* Island, or land by water.
Eia

Eyke   ON *eik.* Place at the oak tree.
Eyk

Fakenham(Magna & Little) OE *Facca* + OE *ham.* Facca's homestead.
Fachenham

Falkenham   OE **Falta* + OE *ham.* *Falta's homestead.
Faltenham

Farnham   OE *fearn* + OE *ham* or *hamm.* Fern   homestead
Ferneham   or water-meadow.

Felixstowe   OE **Filica* + OE *stow.* *Felica's meeting place
Filchestou   or holy place, later associated with East Anglia's
(1254)   first bishop, St Felix.

Felsham   OE *Fæle* + OE *ham.* Fæle's homestead (*fæle* means
Fealsham   'pleasant').

Finborough (Great)   OE *fina* + OE *beorg.* Woodpecker hill.
Fineberga

Finningham   OE **Fina* + OE *ingas* + *ham.*   The homestead
Finingaham   belonging to *Fina's people, or belonging to t h e
      Finborough people.

Flempton   OE *Fleming* + OE *tun.*   Probably farmstead be-
Flemingtuna   longing to the people from Flanders.

Flixton   ON *Flik* + OE *tun.* Flik's farmstead.
Flixtuna

Flowton   OE *Floki* + OE *tun.* Floki's farmstead.
Flochetuna

Fordley   OE *ford* + OE *leah.*   Clearing/wood/pasture by a
Forle   ford.

Fornham (All Saints & St.Martin) OE *forne* + OE *ham.* Homestead
Fornham   where trout are caught. The Fornhams are on both
      sides of the Lark. 'All Saints' and 'St Martin' come
      from the 13th century church dedications.

Framlingham   OE **Framela* + OE *ingas* + *ham.* The homestead
Framelingaham   belonging to *Framela's people.

Framsden   OE *Fram* + OE *denu.* Fram's valley.
Framesdena

Freckenham   OE **Freca* + OE *ham.* *Freca's homestead.
Frakenaham

Fressingfield OE *Frisa* or *fyrs(en)* + OE *(ingas)* + *feld.* Mills
Fessefelda opts for a personal name, **Frisa* (possibly the
(Frisingefeld 1185) Frisian), hence the 'open ground belonging to the
Frisian's people'. Ekwall opts for the furze plant
(presumably because of the Domesday entry) hence
'open ground covered with furze'.

Freston OE *Frisa* + OE *tun.* The Frisian's farmstead.
Fresetuna

Friston OE *Frisa* + OE *tun.* The Frisian's farmstead.
Frisetuna

Fritton OE *frith* or OSc *Frithi* + OE *tun.* It either
Fridetuna means a fenced-in farmstead (offering protection),
or is Frithi's farmstead.

Frostenden OE *frosc* + OE *denu.* Frog valley.
Froxedena

Gazeley OE **Gægi* + OE *leah.* *Gægi's woodland clearing.
Gaysle (1219) clearing.

Gedding OE **Gydda* + OE *ingas.* The place belonging to
Gedinga *Gydda's people.

Gedgrave OE *gata* + OE *graf.* Goats' grove.
Gategraua

Gipping OE *Gyppi* or *Gyppa* + OE *ingas.* The place of
Gippinges Gyppi's people.
(Henry II, 12th C.)

Gisleham OE *Gysela* + OE *ham.* Gysela's homestead.
Gisleham

Gislingham OE *Gysela* + OE *ingas.* The place of Gysela's
Gyselingham people.
(1060)

Glemham (Great & Little) OE *gleam* + OE *ham.* Merriment homestead
Glaimham - perhaps noted for games or revelry.

Glemsford OE *gleam* + OE *ford.* Merriment ford perhaps
Glemesford were people gathered for games. (See **Playford.**)
(1050)

Gosbeck OE *gos* + ON *bekkr.* Goose stream.
Gosebech (1179)

Groton OE **groten* + OE *ea.* Possibly sandy or pebbly
Grotena stream. OE *grot* means a particle and is found in
sandgrot (grain of sand) and *meregrota* (sea
pebble).

Grundisburgh *Grundesburch*	*Grund* + OE *burh*. Stronghold at Grund. Grund was possibly the earlier name of the place and may be identical with OE *grund* meaning 'foundation', possibly referring to an earlier foundation of a building).
Gunton *Guneton (1198)*	OE *Gunni* + OE *tun*. Gunni's farmstead.
Hacheston *Hacestuna*	OE *Hæcci* + OE *tun*. Hæcci's farmstead.
Hadleigh *Hetlega*	OE *hæth* + OE *leah*. Heather clearing.
Halesworth *Healesuurda*	OE **Hæle* + OE *worth*. *Hæle's enclosure.
Hargrave *Haragraua*	OE *hara* or *har* + OE graf. The name either means 'Hare (*hara*) Grove' or 'Grey/Hoar (*har*) Grove'. *Har* is often used in other names in association with things marking boundaries, and some scholars think *har* came to mean boundary, making 'Boundary Grove' a possibility.
Harkstead *Herchesteda*	OE *Hereca* + OE *stede*. Hereca's place or pasture. *Stede* is not often found following a personal name, but a personal name for the first element seems the best solution in this instance.
Harleston *Heroluestuna*	OE *Heoruwulf* or *Herewulf* + OE *tun*. Heoruwulf's or Herewulf's farmstead.
Hartest *Herterst*	OE *heorot* + OE *hyrst*. Stag wood. (*Hyrst* sometimes denoted a hillock.)
Hasketon *Haschetuna*	OE **Haseca* + OE *tun*. *Haseca's farmstead.
Haughley *Hagala*	OE *haga* + OE *leah*. Hawthorn clearing or wood.
Haverhill *Hauerhella*	OE **hæfera* (or ON *hafri*) + OE hyll. Hill where oats are grown.
Hawkedon *Hauokeduna*	OE *hafoc* + OE *dun*. Hawks' Hill.
Hawstead *Haldsteda*	OE *h(e)ald* + OE *stede*. *Hald* could mean 'sloping' or 'refuge'. Possibly place of shelter.
Hazelwood *Haselewood*	OE *hæsel* + OE *wudu*. Hazel wood.

Hawstead *Haldsteda*	OE *h(e)ald* + OE *stede*. *Hald* could mean 'sloping' or 'refuge'. Possibly place of shelter.
Hazelwood *Haselewood*	OE *hæsel* + OE *wudu*. Hazel wood.
Helmingham *Helmingheham*	OE *Helm* + OE *ingas* + *ham*. The homestead of Helm's people.
Hemingstone *Hamingestuna*	ON *Hemingr* + OE *tun*. Hemingr's farmstead.
Hemley *Helmelea*	OE **Helma* + OE *leah*. *Helma's clearing.
Hengrave *Hemegretham*	OE *Hemma* + OE **gred* + *ham*. Hemma's homestead and grassy meadow.
Henham *Henham*	OE *hea(n)* + *ham*. High homestead.
Henley *Henleia*	OE *heah* + OE *leah*. High (or chief) wood or clearing.
Henstead *Henestede*	OE *henn* + OE *stede*. Place frequented by wild birds.
Hepworth *Hepworda*	OE **Heppa* + OE *worth*. Heppa's enclosure. Ekwall suggests *heope* (dog rose) as the first element and interprets the name as 'hedge where hips grow'.
Herringfleet *Herlingaflet*	OE **Herela* + OE *ingas* + *fleot*. The stream of *Herela's people.
Herringswell *Hymingwella*	OE *hyrne* + OE *ing* + *wella*. Place by the spring at the corner of land (*hyrne*). Ekwall argues for *ingas* instead of *ing* (place) - the spring belonging to the people living on the corner of land. There is a horseshoe-shaped ridge near the place.
Hessett *Hetseta*	OE *hecg* + OE *(ge)set*. Hedge fold (for keeping animals).
Heveningham *Heueniggeham*	OE **Hefin* + OE *ingas* + *ham*. The homestead belonging to *Hefin's people.
Higham *Heihham*	OE *heah* + OE *ham*. High (or chief) homestead.
Hinderclay *Hilderclea*	OE **hyldre* + OE *clea*. Tongue of land (*clea* literally means claw) where elder trees grew.

Hintlesham	OE *Hyntel* + OE *ham* or *hamm*. *Hyntel's home-
Hintlesham	stead or water meadow/enclosure.
Hitcham	OE *hecg* or *hecc* + OE *ham*. Homestead with a
Hecham	hedge or hatch-gate.
Holbrook	OE *hol* + OE *broc*. Brook in a hollow or ravine.
Holebroc	
Hollesley	OE *Hol* or *hol* + OE *leah*. Either *Hol's clearing,
Holeslea	or wood/clearing in a hollow.
Holton (St Mary)	OE *Hola* or *hol* + OE *tun*. *Hola's farmstead,
Holetuna	or farmstead near a hollow. 'St Mary' comes from
	the dedication of the church.
Homersfield	OE *Hunbeorht* + OE *feld*. Hunbeorht's open land.
Humbresfelda	
Honington	OE *Hun(a)* + OE *ingas* + *tun*. Farmstead belonging
Hunegetuna	to Huna's people.
Hoo Green	OE *hoh*. Hill-spur.
Hou	
Hopton (nr.Lowestoft)	OE *hop* + OE *tun*. Farmstead with an enclosed
Hoppetuna	plot of land. Although *hop* can mean a small valley,
	it is usually a plot of enclosed land. Gelling argues
	for 'farmstead on a promontory jutting into marsh'
	for the Suffolk Hoptons.
Hopton (nr.Thetford)	OE *hop* + OE *tun*. Farmstead with an enclosed
Hopetuna	plot of land. Although *hop* can mean a small valley,
	it is usually a plot of enclosed land. Gelling argues
	for 'farmstead on a promontory jutting into marsh'
	for the Suffolk Hoptons.
Horham	OE *horh* + OE *ham*. Dirty or muddy homestead.
Horham (c.950)	
Hornham	OE *?horna* + OE *ham*. Presumably, homestead on
	a horn-shaped piece of land.
Horningsheath (Great and Little)	OE *horning* + OE *erth*. Ploughed land
Horningeserda	at the bend in the river. *Horning* means 'bend'
	although it may be the old name of the River Linnet
	meaning 'winding stream'. Alternatively *Horning
	may be a personal name.
Horringer	OE *Horning* or *horning* + OE *erth*. Either
Horningeserda	*Horning's ploughed land, or ploughed land at a
	bend.

Hoxne *Hoxana*	OE*hohsinu. Literally a heel-sinew. The place is on a spur of land between the Waveney and one of its tributaries. If the OE element is correct, the place may have derived its name from the similarity of the shape of the spur to the hough of a horse.
Hundon *Hunedana*	OE *Huna* + OE *denu*. Huna's valley.
Hunston *Hunterstuna*	OE *huntere* + OE *tun*. The farmstead belonging to the hunter.
Huntingfield *Huntingafelda*	OE *Hunta* + OE *ingas* + *feld*. Open land belonging to Hunta's people.
Icklingham *Ecclingaham*	OE **Yccel* + OE *ingas* + *ham*. Homestead belonging to *Yccel's people.
Ickworth *Ikewrth (c.950)*	OE *Ic(c)a* + OE *worth*. Icca's enclosure.
Iken *Ykene*	OE **Ican* + OE *ea*. Possibly *Ica's stream.
Ilketshall (St Lawrence & St Margaret) *Ilcheteleshala*	ON*Ylfketill + OE *halh*. *Ylfketill's corner of land. 'St Lawrence' and 'St Margaret' are from the dedications of the churches.
Ingate Place *Endegat (1201)*	Presumably the place at the gate at the end of the territory
Ingham *Ingham*	OE *Inga* + OE *ham*. Inga's homestead. It has been suggested that the first element may be linked with a Germanic tribe, and may mean 'the Inguoine'.
Ipswich *Gipeswic*	OE *Gip* + OE *wic*. Gip's wic. *Wic* can have a range of meanings from 'dairy-farm' to 'salt-works'. Here Mills gives 'harbour'. Ekwall suggests that there may be a reference to 'harbour' hidden in the first element with possible connections to other words meaning 'gap'.
Ixworth *Giswortha*	OE **Gicsa* or **Gycsa* + OE *worth*. *Gicsa's enclosure.
Ixworth Thorpe *Torp*	OE *Ixworth* + ON *thorp*. Ixworth's secondary settlement.
Kedington *Kidituna* *(Kydington 1043)*	OE *Cydda* + OE *ingas* + *tun*. Farmstead belonging to Cydda's people.

Kelsale *Keleshala*	OE *Ceol* or **Cel(i)* + OE *halh*. Ceol's or *Celi's corner of land.
Kentford *Cheneteforde* *(11th Century)*	OE *Cynete* + OE *ford*. Ford over the River Kennet.
Kenton *Chenetuna*	OE *Cena* or *cyne* + OE *tun*. Either Cena's farm-stead, or royal 'tun' - hence royal manor.
Kentwell *Kanewella* *(Kenetwelle* *1161)*	OE *Cynete* + OE *wella*. Kentwell is not far from the River Glem and may be the old name of the river. If this is true the explanatory 'stream' *(wella)* was added to Cynete.
Kersey *Careseia*	OE *cærse* + OE *eg*. Cress island.
Kesgrave *Gressegraua*	OE *cærse* + OE *græf*. Cress ditch.
Kessingland *Kessingalanda*	OE**Cyssi* + OE *ingas* + *land*. Cultivated land belonging to *Cyssi's people.
Kettlebaston *Kitelbeornastuna*	ON *Ketilbjorn* + OE *tun*. Ketilbjorn's farmstead.
Kettleburgh *Ketelbria*	ON *Ketil* or OE *cetel* + ON *berg* or OE *beorg*. Possibly Ketil's hill, or hill by a narrow valley.
Kirkley *Kirkelea*	ON *kirkja* + OE *leah*. Woodland clearing belonging to a church. As with Kirton, the fact that the ON *kirkja* has been combined with an OE element suggests that it may have replaced an earlier OE *cirice*.
Kirton *Kirketuna*	ON *kirkja* + OE *tun*. Farmstead with a church. As with Kirkley, the fact that the ON *kirkja* has been added to an OE element suggests that it may have replaced an earlier OE *cirice*.
Knettishall *Gnedeshalla*	OE *gnætt* + OE *halh*. Gnat's nook. 'Gnat' may be used as a nickname.
Knodishall *Cnotesheala*	OE *Cnott* + OE *halh*. Cnott's corner of land.
Lackford *Lecforda*	OE *leac* + OE *ford*. Leek ford.

Lakenheath *Lakingahethe*	OE *Laca* or *lacu* + OE *ingas* + *hyth*. The landing-place belonging to Laca's people, or the landing-place belonging to people living by the stream (*lacu*).
Langham *Langham*	OE *lang* + OE *ham* or *hamm*. Long homestead or water meadow/enclosure.
Lark (River)	The river got its name from **Lackford**.
Lavenham *Lauenham*	OE *Lafa* + OE *ham*. Lafa's homestead.
Lawshall *Lawessela*	OE *hlaw* + OE *sele*. Hill dwelling.
Laxfield *Laxefelda*	OE *Leaxa* + OE *feld*. Leaxa's open land.
Layham *Hligham (c.995)*	OE **hlig* + OE *ham*. Homestead with a shelter.
Leiston *Leistuna*	OE *leah* or *leg* + OE *tun*. The first element is unclear. The name could mean 'Farmstead in the clearing'. Given that Leiston is near the coast, 'Beacon-fire (*leg*) farmstead' may be a possibility.
Letheringham *Letheringaham*	OE *Leodhere* + OE *ingas* + *ham*. Homestead belonging to Leodhere's people.
Levington *Leuentona*	OE *Leofa* + OE *tun*. Leofa's farmstead.
Lidgate *Litgata*	OE *hlid-geat*. Swing-gate.
Lindsey *Lealeseia*	OE **Lelli* + OE *eg*. *Lelli's island.
Linstead (Magna & Parva) *Linestede*	OE *lin* or *hlyn* + OE *stede*. Place where flax (*lin*) or maples-trees (*hlyn*) grow. 'Magna' and 'Parva' are Latin affixes for 'Great' and 'Little'.
Livermere (Great) *Leuuremer*	OE **lifer* + OE *mere*. The first element is uncertain. The name may mean 'pool with thick, muddy water', or simply 'liver-shaped pool'.
Loudham *Ludeham*	OE *Hluda* + OE *ham*. Hluda's homestead. Hluda is derived from *hlud* (loud).
Lound *Lunda*	ON *lundr*. Small wood.

Lowestoft *Lothu Wistoft* *(Lothewistoft 1212)*	ON *Hlothver* + ON *toft*. Hlothver's plot of land.
Marlesford *Merlesforda*	OE **Mærel* + OE *ford*. *Mærel's ford. Ekwall points out that Marlesford is only two miles from Martley and may simply mean 'Martley Ford'.
Martlesham *Merelesham*	OE *mearth* or **Mertel* + OE *leah* + *ham*. Homestead in Marten Wood, or a possibility of Martel's clearing.
Martley *Mertlega*	OE *mearth* + OE *leah*. Marten Wood.
Melford (Long) *Melaforda*	OE *mylen* + OE *ford*. Mill ford.
Mellis *Mellels*	OE *mylen*. The mills.
Mells *Mealla*	OE *mylen*. The mills.
Melton *Meltuna*	ON *mythal* or OE *mæl* or OE *mylen* + OE *tun*. Both Ekwall and Mills are agreed that in most Meltons the first element is 'middle' (*mythal*), but that in this case it could be *mæl* giving the name meaning 'farmstead with a crucifix'. *Mylen* (mill) has also been suggested.
Mendham *Mendham* *(Myndham c.950)*	OE **Mynda* + OE *ham*. *Mynda's homestead.
Mendlesham *Mundlesham*	OE **Myndel* + OE *ham*. *Myndel's homestead.
Metfield *Medefeld (1214)*	OE *mæd* + OE *feld*. Open land meadow.
Mettingham *Metingaham*	OE *Metti* + OE *ingas* + *ham*. The homestead belonging to Metti's people.
Mickfield *Mucelfelda*	OE *micel* + OE *feld*. Large area of open country.
Middleton *Mideltuna*	OE *middel* + OE *tun*. Middle farmstead.
Milden *Mellinga*	OE *melde* or **Melda* + OE *ingas* or *ing*. Either 'place where orach (goosefoot family) grows', or 'the place belonging to *Melda's people'.

Mildenhall
Mildenhale

OE *middel* or **Milda* + OE *halh*. Either 'middle corner of land' or '*Milda's corner of land'.

Minsmere
Mensemara

ON *mynni* + OE *mere*. River-mouth pool.

Monewden
Munegadena

OE **Munda* + OE *ingas* + *denu*. The valley belonging to **Munda's people.

Monk Soham
Saham

OE *sae* + OE *ham*. Homestead by the pool, with early possession by the monks at Bury St Edmunds.

Monks Eleigh
Illeleia
(Monkesillegh 1304)

OE **Illa* + OE *leah*. **Illa's clearing in the wood. The ME *munuc* means 'belonging to a *monk'* and alludes to ownership by St Paul's in London.

Moulton
Muletuna

OE *mul* or *Mula* + OE *tun*. Either 'Mule farmstead', or 'Mula's farmstead'.

Mutford
Mutford

OE *(ge)motford*. Ford at which moots (meetings) were held.

Nacton
Nachetuna

ON *Hnaki* or *Nokkvi* + OE *tun*. Hnaki's or Nokkvi's farmstead.

Naughton
Nawelton (c.1150)

?ON *Nagli* + OE *tun*. Possibly Nagli's farmstead, although the first element is uncertain.

Nayland
Eilanda
(Neiland 1227)

OE *eg-land*. (Place at the) island. The N came from the ME 'atten' (at the).

Nedging (Tye)
Niedinga
(Hnyddinge c.995)

OE **Hnydda* + OE *ing*. **Hnydda's place. 'Tye' is a later affix meaning common pasture.

Needham Market
Nedham (13 Century)
Nedeham Markett (1511)

OE *nied* + OE *ham*. Needy homestead.

Nettlestead
Nettlesteda

OE *netele* + OE *stede*. Place where nettles grow.

Newbourn
Neubrunna

OE *niwe* + OE *burna*. New stream (almost certainly referring to a change of course).

Newmarket
Novum Forum (1200)
Novum Mercatum (1219)
la Newmarket (1418)

L *novum* + L *forum*. New market place. The ME 'New' and 'Market' have replaced the Latin of the earliest forms.

Newton	OE *niwe* + OE *tun*. New farmstead.
Northale	OE *north* + ?OE *halh*. Possibly northern corner of land.
Norton *Nortuna*	OE *north* + OE *tun*. North farmstead.
Nowton *Neotuna* *(Newetune c.950)*	OE *niwe* + OE *tun*. New farmstead.
Oakley *Acle*	OE *ac* + OE *leah*. Oak wood.
Occold *Acholt*	OE *ac* + OE *holt*. Oak wood.
Offton *Offetuna*	OE *Offa* + OE *tun*. Offa's farmstead.
Old Newton *Neweton (1196)*	OE *niwe* + OE *tun*. New farmstead.
Onehouse *Anuhus*	OE *an* + OE *hus*. Single or isolated dwelling.
Orford *Oreford (1164)*	OE *ora* + OE *ford*. Ford near the shore.
Otley *Otelaga*	OE **Otta* + OE *leah*. *Otta's woodland clearing.
Oulton *Aleton (1203)*	ON *Ali* or OE *ald* + OE *tun*. Either 'Ali's farmstead' or 'old farmstead'. This should not be confused with the Oulton in Norfolk which was probably associated with the ON personal name Authulfr.
Ousden *Uuesdana*	OE *uf* + OE *denu*. Owls' valley.
Pakefield *Paggefella*	OE **Pacca* + OE *feld*. *Pacca's open land.
Pakenham *Pachenham*	OE **Pacca* + OE *ham*. *Pacca's homestead.
Palgrave *Palegrave (1035)*	OE ?*pala* + OE *graf*. Possibly grove where poles are obtained.
Parham *Perreham*	OE ?*peru* + OE *ham*. Probably pear homestead.

Peasenhall	OE *pisen* + OE *halh*. Nook where peas grow.
Pisehalla	
Pettaugh	OE *Peota* + OE *haga*. Peota's enclosure.
Petehaga	
Pettistree	OE *Peohtred* + OE *treow*. Peohtred's tree.
Petrestre (1253)	
Playford	OE *plega* + OE *ford*. Sports'/Games' ford.
Plegeforda	(See **Glemsford.**)
Polstead	OE *pol* + OE *stede*. Place by the pool.
Polesteda	
Poslingford	OE **Possel* + OE *ingas* + *worth*. The enclosure
Poslingeorda	of *Possel's people.
(Poselingwrtha 1195)	
Preston	OE *preost* + OE *tun*. Priests' farmstead.
Prestetona	
Ramsholt	OE *hramsa* + OE *holt*. Wild garlic wood. There
Ramesholt	is a possibility that the first element could be *ramm* which would make the meaning 'ram wood'.
Rattlesden	OE ? + OE *denu*. The first element is obscure,
Ratesdana	but is probably an unknown personal name
Ratlesdena	or nickname. Whoever (s)he was, (s)he lived in a valley. Most wise scholars have refrained from guessing what the name might have been in this case.
Raydon	OE *ryge* + OE *dun*. Rye hill.
Rienduna	
Rede	OE *hreod* or **reod*. Place at the reed bed or
Reoda	clearing.
Redgrave	OE *hreod* or *read* + OE *græf* or *graf*. Either 'reed
Redgrafe	trench/pit' or 'red grove'.
(11th Century)	
Redisham	OE **Read* + OE *ham*. *Read's homestead. The
Redesham	possessive form '-is' suggests a personal name instead of *hreod* or *read*. (See **Redgrave**).
Redlingfield	OE *Rædel* or *Rædla* + OE *ingas* + *feld*. Open
Radlinghefelda	land belonging to Rædel's or Rædla's people.
Rendham	OE *rymed* or **rind(e)* + OE *ham*. Either 'cleared
Rimdham	homestead' or 'hill homestead'.
Rindham	

Rendlesham
mansio Rendili (c.730)
OE *Rendel* + OE *ham*. Rendel's homestead.

Reydon
Rienduna
OE *rygen* + OE *dun*. Rye hill.

Rickinghall (Inferior & Superior) OE **Rica* + OE *ingas* + *halh*.
Rikingahala
Corner of land owned by *Rica's people.

Ringsfield
Ringesfelda
OE**Hring* (ON Hringr) or *hring* + OE *feld*.
Either '*Hring's open land', or 'open land with a circular feature'.

Ringshall
Ringeshala
OE **Hring* (ON *Hringr*) or *hring* + OE *halh*.
Either '*Hring's corner of land', or 'corner of land with a circular feature'.

Risby
Risebi
ON *hris* or + ON *by*. Either 'brushwood farmstead' or 'farmstead in the clearing'.

Rishangles
Risangra
OE *hris* + OE *hangra*. Brushwood slope.

Rougham Green
Ruhham
OE *ruh* + OE *ham*. Homestead on rough ground.

Roydon Drift
Rigindun (995)
OE *ryge* + OE *dun*. Rye hill.

Rumburgh
Ramburc
OE *rum* or *run* or *hruna* + OE *burh*. There was clearly a stronghold (*burh*). It was either wide (*rum*), made of trunks (*hruna*), or used for council meetings (*run*). 'Wide' seems the most likely as all burhs would be made of trunks.

Rushbrooke
Ryscebroc
OE *rysc* + OE *broc*. Rushes' brook.

Rushmere (St Andrew) OE *rysc* + OE *mere*. Rushes' pool ('St Andrew'
Ryscemara
from the dedication of the church).

Santon Downham
Dunham
OE *sand* + *tun* + OE *dun* + *ham*. Santon means 'farmstead on sandy soil', Downham means 'hill homestead'. The *dun-ham* is used to distinguish Santon from the nearby one in Norfolk.

Sapiston
Sapestuna
OE *?saperes* + OE *tun*. Possibly 'the soap-maker's farmstead', although Hill suggests that the first element is likely to be an unknown personal name.

Saxham (Great & Little) OE *Seax* + OE *ham*. The Saxons' homestead.
    Saxham

Saxmundham   OE *Seaxmund + OE *ham*. *Seaxmund's homestead.
    Sasmundeham

Saxstead   OE ?*Seaxa* + OE *stede*. Probably Seaxa's place.
    Saxsteda

Semer   OE *sæ* + OE *mere*. Lake lake. *Sæ* could mean 'sea'
    Seamera   as well as 'lake', but 'mere' was probably added to
       Sæ when the sense of 'lake' was lost.

Shadingfield   OE ?*scead* + *denu*, or *scaden* + OE *feld*. Ekwall
    Scadenafella   suggests 'open land *(feld)* near the boundary valley
       (scead + denu). However 'separated *(scaden)* open
       land' is a possibility. It is near Hundred River on the
       hundred boundary and 'boundary' is stated or
       implicit in both possibilities.

Shelland   OE *scylf* + OE *land*. Land on a slope or ledge.
    Sellanda

Shelley   OE *scylf* + OE *leah*. Clearing on a slope or ledge.
    Sceueleia

Shimpling   OE *Scimpel + OE *ingas*. (The settlement) of
    Simplinga   *Scimpel's people.

Shipmeadow   OE *sceap* + OE *mæd*. Sheep meadow.
    Scipmedu

Shotley   OE *sceote or *sceot* + OE *leah*. Either 'pigeon
    Scoteleia   wood/clearing' or 'shooting wood/clearing'.

Shottisham   OE *Sceot or *Scot* + OE *ham*. *Sceot's or
    Scotesham   Scot's homestead.

Shrubland   OE *scrybb* + ON *lundr*. Shrub grove.
    Shrubblund (1301)

Sibton   OE *Sibba* + OE *tun*. Sibba's farmstead.
    Sibbetuna

Sizewell   OE *Sigehere* + OE *wella*. Sigehere's spring.
    Syreswell (1240)

Snape   OE *snæp* or ON *snap*. Probably 'boggy piece of
    Snapes   land' or 'poor pasture'.

Soham   See **Earl Soham, Monk Soham.**

Somerleyton   ON *Sumarlithi* + OE *tun*. Sumarlithi's farmstead.
    Sumerledetuna

Somersham *Sumersham*	OE **Sumor* + OE *ham.* *Sumor's homestead.
Somerton *Sumerledetuna*	ON *Sumarlithi* + OE *tun.* Sumarlithi's farmstead. Normally Somertons means 'farmsteads used in the summer', but in this case *Sumarlithi* is present in the early spellings. (See **Somerleyton**.)
Sotherton *Sudretuna*	OE *sutherra* + OE *tun.* Southern farmstead.
Sotterley *Soterlega*	OE *?* + OE *leah.* The first element is obscure, but is probably an unknown personal name or nickname. Whoever (s)he was, (s)he lived in a woodland clearing. Most wise scholars have refrained from guessing what the name might have been in this case.
Southolt *Sudholda*	OE *suth* + OE *holt.* South wood.
Southwold *Sudwolda*	OE *suth* + OE *wald.* South forest.
Spexhall *Specteshale (1197)*	OE **speoht* + OE *halh.* Woodpeckers' Corner.
Sproughton *Sproeston*	OE *Sprow* + OE *tun.* Sprow's farmstead.
Stanningfield *Stanfelda*	OE *stan* or *stanen* + OE *feld.* Stony ground. The '-ing' in modern spelling is absent from early spellings and is misleading. It tempts one to fall into the trap of 'the ground belonging to Stan's people'.
Stansfield *Stanesfelda*	OE **Stan* + OE *feld.* Probably '*Stan's open ground'. The first element could be *stan* (stone). However, the possessive form '-es' suggests a personal name.
Stanstead *Stanesteda*	OE *stan* + OE *stede.* Stony place.
Stanton *Stantuna*	OE *stan* + OE *tun.* Stony farmstead.
Sternfield *Sternesfelda*	OE **Sterne* + OE *feld.* Probably Sterne's open ground.
Stoke (Ash & by Nayland) *Stoches (Ash)* *Stoches (Clare)* *Stoc c.970 (Nayland)*	OE *stoc.* Outlying farmstead, secondary settlement. 'Ash' most probably refers to a tree. 'Clare' and 'Nayland' are nearby settlements.

Stonham (Aspall, Earl & Little) OE *stan* + OE *ham*. Homestead on
Stanham   stony ground. Stonham Aspell was held by Roger
            de Aspale in 1292. Rogerus Bigod of Earl Stonham
            is mentioned in 1212.

Stoven   OE/ON *stofn*. (Place at the) tree stump(s).
Stouone

Stow (West)   OE *stow*. Place, inhabited place, or possibly holy
Stowa   place.

Stowlangtoft   OE *stow*. Inhabited place. The manor was held by
Stou   Richard de Langetot in 1206. Langetot is a common
         Norman name.

Stowmarket   OE *stow*. Place, possibly meeting place. Stow
Stou   is the name of the hundred. 'Market' had been added
         by 1253. An earlier name for the place was
         Thorney.

Stowupland   ?OE *stow* + OE *upp* + ?OE *land*. Possibly   the
                 meeting or religious site on the upper part of the
                 land/estate.

Stradbroke   OE *?stræt* + OE *broc*. Possibly brook by a paved
Statebroc   road.
(Stradebroc 1168)

Stradishall   OE *stræt* + OE *gesell*. Shelter on the road.
Stratesella

Stratford (St.Andrew & St.Mary) OE *stræt* + OE *ford*. Ford where a
Straffort   Roman road crossed a river. ('St Andrew' and 'St
(St Andrew)   Mary' are from the dedications of the churches.)
Stratfort (St.Mary)

Stuston   OE **Stut* + OE *tun*. *Stut's farmstead. The posses-
Stutestuna   sive form '-es' suggests a personal name. (See
               Stutton.)

Stutton   OE *stut* or ON *stutr* + OE *tun*. Either 'gnat farm-
Stuttuna   stead' or 'bullock farmstead'.

Sudbourne   OE *suth* + OE *burna*. South stream.
Sutburna

Sudbury   OE *suth* + OE *burg*. Southern fortified settlement.
Sutberia

Suffolk   OE *suth* + OE *folc*. The Southern People.
Sudfulc

Sutton	OE *suth* + OE *tun*. South farmstead.	
Suthtuna		
Sweffling	OE **Swiftel* + OE *ingas*. (The place of)	
Sueflinga	*Swiftel's people.	
Swilland	OE *swin* + OE *land*. Land where pigs are	
Suinlanda	kept.	
Syleham	OE *?sylu* or *?sulh* + OE *ham*. Possibly homestead	
Seilam	by a miry place' or perhaps 'homestead in a gully'.	
Tannington	OE *Tata* + OE *ingas* + *tun*. The farmstead	
Tatintuna	belonging to Tata's people.	
Tattingstone	OE **Tating* + OE *tun*. Probably *Tating's farm-	
Tatistuna	stead'.	
(Tatingeston 1219)		
Theberton	OE *Theodbeorht* + OE *tun*. Theodbeorht's farm-	
Thewardetuna	stead.	
Thelnetham	OE *thel* + *elfitu* + OE *hamm*. Possibly water	
Thelueteham	meadow/enclosure (*hamm*) frequented by swans	
	(*elfitu*) near a plank bridge (*thel*).	
Thingoe (hundred)	ON *thing* + ON *haugr*. An assembly mound or	
Thingehov	hill.	
Thorington	OE *thorn/thyrne* + OE *tun*. Thorn-tree farmstead.	
Toretuna		
Thorndon	OE *thorn* + OE *dun*. Thorn-tree hill.	
Tornduna		

Thorney (see Stowmarket) OE *thorn* + OE *eg*. Thorn island.

Thornham (Magna & Parva) OE *thorn* + OE *ham*. Thorn-tree home-
*Thornham*stead.   'Magna' is Latin for 'Great', and 'Parva' is Latin for
'Little'.

Thorpe (Common & Morieux) ON *thorp*. Outlying farmstead or hamlet.
Torpa (Common)   Thorpe Morieux was held by Roger de Murious
Thorp (Morieux)   de Murious in 1201.
1330

Thrandeston	ON *Thrandr* + OE *tun*. Thrandr's farmstead.	
Thrandestuna		

Thurlow (Great & Little) OE *?thryth* + OE *hlaw*. Possibly, 'warriors' burial
Tridlauua   mound'. If the first element is *thryth*, the word could
mean 'noble' as well as 'a troop of warriors'.

Thurston	ON *Thori* + OE *tun*. Thori's farmstead.	
Thurstuna		

Thwaite	ON *thveit*. A clearing, meadow, or paddock.
Theyt (1228)	
Timworth	OE *Tima* + OE *worth*. Tima's enclosure.
Timeworda	
Tostock	OE **tot* + OE *stoc*. A look-out (*tot*) place. The
Totestoc	place is on a hill.

Trimley (St Martin & St Mary) OE **Trymma* + OE *leah*. *Trymma's
Tremelaia   clearing. 'St Martin' and 'St Mary' are from the
                     dedication of the churches.

Troston	OE **Trosta* + OE *ingas* + *tun*. The farmstead
Trostuna	belonging to *Trosta's people.
(Trostingtun c.1000)	

Tuddenham (St Martin & St Mary) OE *Tuda* + OE *ham*. Tuda's home-
Todenham   stead. 'St Martin' and 'St Mary' come from the
                     dedications of the churches.

Tunstall	OE *tun* + OE *steall*. Farmstead site.
Tunestal	
Ubbeston (Green)	ON *Ubbi* + OE *tun*. Ubbi's farmstead.
Upbestuna	
Ufford	OE *Uffa* + OE *worth*. Uffa's enclosure.
Uffeworda	
Uggeshall	OE **Uggeca* + OE *halh*. *Uggeca's corner of land.
Uggiceheala	
Wade	OE *(ge)wæd*. Ford.
Wada (1165)	
Walberswick	OE **Walbert* + OE *wic*. *Walbert's dairy farm.
Walberdeswike	Although Walbert is uncertain in OE, it is similar
	to the Old German names Waldiberht and
	Walhberht.

Waldingfield (Great & Little) OE *wald* + OE *ingas* + *feld*. Open land
Waldingefelda   belonging to the forest people.
(Wealdingafeld)

Waldringfield	OE *Waldhere* + OE *ingas* + *feld*. Open land
Waldringafelda	belonging to Waldhere's people.
Walpole	OE *walh* (from *wala*) + OE *pol*. The Britons' pool.
Walepola	
Walsham-le-Willows	OE *Walh* or *Wæls* + OE *ham*. Walh's or Waels's
Wal(e)sam	homestead (in the willow trees).

Walton *Waletuna*	OE *walh* (from *wala*) + OE *tun*. The Britons' farmstead

Wangford (Southwold) OE *wang* + OE *ford*. Ford by an open field.
Wankeforda Wangford Green was all open common until 1817.

Wangford (Thetford) OE *wægn* + OE *ford*. Ford that could be crossed
Wamforda with a wagon.
(Wainford 1197)

Wantisden *Wantesdena*	OE *Want* + OE *denu*. Want's valley.
Washbrook *Wasebroc*	OE *wæsce* + OE *broc*. Stream for washing (sheep or clothes).
Wattisfield *Watlesfelda*	OE **Wacol* or **Hwætel* + OE *feld*. *Wacol's or *Hwætel's open ground.
Wattisham *Wecesham*	OE **Wæcci* + OE *ham*. *Wæcci's homestead.
Waveney (River) *Wahenhe (1275)*	OE **wagen* + OE *ea*. Bog river.

Wenham (Great & Little) OE ?**wynn* + OE *ham* or *hamm*. Possibly
Wenham 'homestead with pasture (**wynn*)' or 'water meadow/ enclosure with pasture'.

Wenhaston *Wenadestuna*	OE **Wynhæth* + OE *tun*. *Wynhæth's farmstead.
Wentford *Wanteforda (1115)*	ME *wente* + OE *ford*. Passage ford.
West Stow *Stowa (Westowe 1254)*	OE *stow*. Westerly place.
Westerfield *Westrefelda*	OE **wester* or *westerra* + OE *feld*. (More) westerly open land.
Westhall *Westhala*	OE *west* + OE *halh*. Westerly corner of land.
Westhorpe *Westtorp*	ON *vestr* + OE *thorp*. Westerly outlying farmstead.
Westleton *Westledestuna*	ON *Vestlithi* + OE *tun*. Vestlithi's homestead.
Westley *Westlea*	OE *west* + OE *leah*. Westerly wood or clearing.
Weston *Westuna*	OE *west* + OE *tun*. Westerly farmstead.

Wetherden
Wederdena

OE *wether* + OE *denu.* Valley where wether-sheep (castrated rams) are kept. The first element also occurs in **Wetherley** (Cambridgeshire), **Weatheroak** (Worcester-shire), and **Wetheral** (Cumbria).

Wetheringsett
Wederingaseta

OE ?*Wetherden* + OE *ingas* + *(ge)set.* Probably 'fold belonging to the people from Wetherden'.

Weybread
Weibrada

OE *weg* + OE *brædu.* Broad stretch of land by a (Roman) road.

Whatfield
Watefelda

OE *hwæte* + OE *feld.* Open land where wheat is grown.

Whelnetham (Great & Little)
Hvelfiham

OE ?*hweol* + *elfitu* + OE *hamm.* Ekwall suggests 'an enclosure or water meadow (*hamm*) for swans (*elfitu*)' and that *hweol* has been added to distinguish the place from Thelnetham. The *hweol* literally means 'wheel' and could refer to a water-wheel, or some other circular feature.

Whepstead
Heupestede
(Wepstede 942)

OE **hwip(p)e* + OE *stede.* Brushwood place.

Wherstead
Weruesteda

OE *hwearf* + OE *stede.* Shore (wharf) place.

Whitton
Widituna

OE *Hwita* or *hwit* + OE *tun.* Either 'Hwita's farmstead' or 'White Farmstead'.

Wickham Market
Wikham

OE *wic* + OE *ham.* Homestead associated with a 'vicus' (an earlier Romano-British settlement - possibly a dairy farm). The affix 'Market' is from the development of an important market at the settlement.

Wickham Skeith
Wichamm
(Wicham Skeyth 1368)

OE *wic* + OE *ham.* Homestead associated with a 'vicus' (an earlier Romano-British settlement - possibly a dairy farm). The ON affix 'Skeith' means a race-course.

Wickhambrook
Wichambrok

OE *wic* + OE *ham* + *broc.* Homestead near a brook associated with a 'vicus' (an earlier Romano-British settlement - possibly a dairy farm).

Wilby
Wilebey

OE **willig* + OE *beag.* A circle (*beag*) of willow trees.

Willingham
Wellingaham

OE *Willa* + OE *ingas* + *ham*. Homestead belonging to Willa's people.

Willisham
Wilagesham (1198)

OE *Wiglaf* + OE *ham*. Wiglaf's homestead.

Wingfield
Wighefelda

OE *Wiga* or *wig* + OE *ingas* + *feld*. Probably open land belonging to Wiga's people. Alternatively the first element may derive from OE *weoh* meaning a heathen temple.

Winston
Winestuna

OE *Wine* + OE *tun*. Wine's farmstead.

Wissett
Wisseta
(Witseta 1165)

OE *Witta* or *?witha* + OE *(ge)set*. There is agreement that the second element is 'a fold'. For the first For the first element Mills suggests a personal name. Ekwall suggests *withe* (willow stick), for making the fold. The latter has a common sense appeal, even though the spelling evidence is thin.

Wissington
Wiswythetun
(c.995)

OE *Wigswith* + OE *tun*. Wigswith's (a woman) farmstead.

Withersdale
Weresdel
(Wideresdala 1184)

OE *wether* + OE *dæl*. Valley where wether-sheep (castrated rams) are kept. (See **Wetherden**.)

Withersfield
Wedresfelda

OE *wether* + OE *feld*. Open land where wether-sheep (castrated rams) are kept. (See **Wetherden**.)

Witnesham
Witdesham
(Witnesham 1254)

OE **Wittin* + OE *ham*. *Wittin's homestead.

Wixoe
Wlteskeou
(Widekeshoo 1205)

OE *Widuc* + OE *hoh*. Widuc's hill-spur.

Woodbridge
Wudebrige

OE *wudu* + OE *brycg*. 'Bridge near the wood' or 'wooden bridge'.

Woolpit
Wlfpeta

OE *wulf* + OE *pytt*. Wolf pit (for trapping).

Woolverstone
Uluerestuna

OE *Wulfhere* + OE *tun*. Wulfhere's farmstead.

Wordwell
Wridewella

OE **wride* or *wrid* + OE *wella*. Either 'twisting stream' or 'thicket by a stream'. An early name for the River Lark.

Worlingham *Werlingaham*	OE *Werel* + OE *ingas* + *ham*. The homestead of *Werel's people.
Worlington *Wirilintona* *(Wridelingeton* *1201)*	OE *wride* or *Wordwell* + OE *wella* + *ing* + *tun*, or *ingas* + tun. If Mills is right, it means 'Farmstead by the winding stream'. However, there is also a possibility of 'Farmstead belonging to Wordwell's people'.
Worlingworth *Wyrlingwortha*	OE *Wilhere* + OE *ingas* + *worth*. The enclosure belonging to Wilhere's people.
Wortham *Wortham*	OE *worth* + OE *ham*. Homestead with an enclosure.
Wratting (Great & Little) *Wratinga*	OE *wrætt* + OE *ing*. Place where crosswort or hellebore grows.
Wrentham *Wretham* *(Wrentham 1228)*	OE *Wrenta* + OE *ham*. *Wrenta's homestead. Wrenta may be a nickname meaning 'sulky'.
Wyverstone *Wiuerthestune*	OE *Wigferth* + OE *tun*. Wigferth's farmstead.
Yaxley *Jacheslea*	OE *geac* + OE *leah*. Cuckoo wood.
Yoxford *Gokesford*	OE *geoc* + OE *ford*. Literally 'yoke ford'. Ford wide enough for a yoke of oxen.

42

List 1 - Place-names which indicate Plants and Trees

Alderton
Ashbocking
Ashby
Badwell Ash
Barton
Benacre
Benfield
Benhall
Bentley
Boxford
Boxted
Bramfield
Bramford
Brampton
Brandon
Brome
Bromeswell
Campsea Ash
Copdock
Cornard
Elmham
Elmsett
Elmswell
Eyke
Farnham
Hadleigh
Haughley
Haverhill
Hazelwood

Hinderclay
Kersey
Kesgrave
Lackford
Linstead
? Milden
Nettlestead
Oakley
Occold
Parham
Peasenhall
? Ramsholt
? Redgrave
Reydon
Rishangles
Roydon
Rushbrooke
Rushmere
Shrubland
Stoven
Thorington
Thorndon
Thorney
Thornham
Whatfield
Whepstead
Wilby
Wratting

List 2. Place-names which indicate Animal Life

? Braiseworth
Bricett
Cattawade
Cranley
Cransford
Elveden
Finborough
Fornham
Frostenden
Gosbeck
Hartest
Hawkedon
Henstead

Knettishall
? Moulton
Ousden
? Shotley
Spexhall
Stutton
Swilland
Thelnetham
Wetherden
Withersdale
Withersfield
Woolpit
Yaxley

List 3. Names which include Old Norse elements.

Ashby
Barnby
Bildeston
Blackthorpe
Ellough
Eyke
Flixton
Gosbeck
Hemingstone
Ixworth Thorpe
Kettlebaston
Kettleburgh
Kirkley
Kirton
Lound
Lowestoft
Melton
Minsmere
Nacton

Naughton
? Oulton
Risby
Shrubland
? Snape
Somerleyton
Somerton
? Stoven
? Stutton
Thingoe
Thorpe
Thrandeston
Thurston
Thwaite
Ubbeston
Westhorpe
Westleton
Wickham Skeith